I0464654

Business Ideas

100 Starting Points to Make Money in the New Economy

By Chad Grills

Table of Contents

– 1 –

Introduction

What Do Businesses Look Like When They First Startup?

"A journey of a thousand miles begins with a single step."
–Lao Tau

"The whole thing seemed pretty iffy at that stage, there wasn't really anything except for a guy with a barking laugh building desks out of doors in a converted garage."
–Shel Kaphan, first Amazon CTO, discussing joining Amazon with Jeff Bezos

The term "business" can be tricky. Businesses don't start when you get business cards, file for an LLC, or plan over coffee. I think about businesses like this: they have the potential to begin from a string of good ideas. If the ideas are properly valued and the person coming up with them continues the practice of generating more and better ideas, the business has a chance to live and breathe. Once you begin offering a service or product to others who compensate you for the value you create, the business has officially begun.

Thanks to the Internet, there are more ways than ever to learn about entrepreneurship. But the real learning begins when we set up stakes and incentives, and squeeze ourselves until we take action.

This book contains 100 businesses ideas that could each be started today. The goal of this book and these business ideas is to help build your creative or business "fitness." Part of that fitness is developing an abundant mindset. That's why there aren't 7, 30, or even 50 business ideas here; there are 100. The end results of successful businesses we see every day in the news were never started from just a single idea. They were started, grown, and finally succeeded only after a succession of hundreds, thousands, sometimes tens of thousands of ideas. This concept of idea generation is so important, yet overlooked in our modern world. Nietzsche famously said,

"In reality, the imagination of the good artist or thinker produces continuously good, mediocre or bad things, but his judgment, trained and sharpened to a fine point, rejects, selects, connects... All great artists and thinkers are great workers, indefatigable not only in inventing, but also in rejecting, sifting, transforming, ordering."

What Nietzsche and every great business tycoon have known is that they had to develop the ability to have an endless stream of ideas. One idea wasn't going to cut it. It was only after developing the mental fitness to generate, select and properly order their ideas that they were they able to get fit.

When you're in great business shape, you have so many

ideas and it's hard to value or use them appropriately. You let go of the mindset that great ideas are scarce. You recognize that if you're going to start a business you must be ready to solve any problem, at any time. It's in this zen-like state of "business shape" that you'll be able to utilize ideas. The ideas presented in this book can definitely be successfully implemented, but my hope is that these ideas will help spark a series of your own ideas – ideas that are perfectly suited to wherever you're at in life.

This list of 100 business ideas is designed to build that fitness needed to ideate, reject, order and sift through ideas. By mixing them with your own experiences, skills and ambitions, I believe you'll stumble onto something amazing. If you blend that with taking massive action and never stop coming up with great ideas, there is no stopping you.

All these ideas are just starting points. They can be modified (and should be) however we see fit. The goal is to just begin, and get our entrepreneurial muscles working immediately. We can look at the ideas below as businesses, experiments, micro-businesses, or incentivized experiments with stakes. What matters most is that we get started so that we can get learning.

A Caveat about the Sharing Economy

The mainstream media and most of the technology industry love the phrase "sharing economy." This is an annoying phrase on a few different levels, mainly because we're not sharing anything; the market for everything has just become more liquid. Technology has lowered search costs and allowed people to do business with one another much more easily. These people aren't sharing anything; they're buying and selling goods and services (albeit temporarily). Just because the mainstream media turns its nose up to what business looks like on a small or local level doesn't mean we have to use the language and terms they give us. The "sharing economy" is a blessing to anyone who wants to build his or her entrepreneurial muscle. It's an opportunity for each of us to start businesses more easily and create value in the economy for everyone else along the way.

The platforms and businesses that have helped make the economy more liquid, such as AirBnb, Lyft, Uber, and even DogVacay, allow us to become instantly more entrepreneurial. We can begin the learning curve today and get paid to learn the right things. These types of businesses provide anyone the opportunity to start their own micro-business immediately, on a marketplace platform that is continually being perfected to please both parties involved. This opportunity is in stark contrast to most MBA and entrepreneurship programs where we pay to study often outdated business case studies. This formalized style of education and college training is certainly socially acceptable and perhaps easier to explain or justify to our family. But all the ideas below put us on the path of real learning. They all are designed to spark ideas or invite us to take the real actions necessary to learn about business and entrepreneurship. The best lessons and learning we'll always remember comes only through practice. All the 100 ideas below are about practicing and about making money, instead of paying to study old examples.

Many people don't take their business ideas seriously enough because they forget the humble nature from which all businesses grow. This is natural and to be expected. After all, traditional media focuses most on the polished end product of entrepreneurs. They often leave out the humble beginnings that all of us are capable of achieving today. Before we jump into the list of 100 business ideas, let's briefly review how a few well-known entrepreneurs first got their start.

How Did They Get Started?

"That's sort of the beauty of creating it. It often takes the act of creating it for the idea to emerge. Often it's not there at the very beginning."
–Kevin Kelly

- **Aaron Levie**, CEO of Box.com: Started many small web design businesses and experiments.
- **Tracy DiNunzio**, CEO of Tradesy.com: Rented out her apartment via AirBnb to make extra cash while she was learning and building what became Tradesy.
- **Ilan Zechory**, Co-Founder of Genius.com: Started selling his services as a licensed hypnotist before co-founding what became Genius.
- **Richard Branson**, Founder of The Virgin Group: Started selling advertising space in a magazine he started before the magazine actually existed.
- **Marc Cuban**, Founder of many companies including Broadcast.com. Now Cuban is a VC on Shark Tank, Creator of CyberDust and Expire, as well as other products and apps. Cuban got his start in business through bartending, selling powdered milk door to door, and then learning about software by selling

software. After he had been fired from his job selling software, he started a computer servicing company to fix all the problems he saw at his previous employer.

- **Tim Ferriss**, Author, and Angel Investor: Got his start with a conference for speed reading and an audio program about how to get into an Ivy League College; then he started a business selling a single workout supplement through website, phone, and mail orders.
- **Travis Kalanick**, CEO of Uber: Got his start with a business he founded with a neighbor. They tutored large groups of students for the SAT.

The examples of small starts are everywhere. The difference between those which started small and stayed small versus those which started small and grew large is only mindset.

When someone pays us for a product or service we render, we make his or her life better. At that moment, we arc doing our part to rebuild America. That gap between the cost of what we create and the value it brings to someone else (our margin) is real philanthropy at its core. There isn't anything more American than creating value where none previously existed.

Creating businesses is also a fantastic mental and financial insurance policy. When we know we can start with nothing and build multiple income streams, we gain a rare type of confidence. There are few things more satisfying than knowing we can lose everything we have yet still find a way to make money.

We open more options to ourselves by cultivating the ability to start businesses. Once we've built that entrepreneurial skill, we can be dropped anywhere in the United States and within a few months be up and running, making money by moving resources from areas of lower yield to higher yield. This is the ultimate optionality and freedom. There isn't a better path to crushing our own fears.

There is no reason to wait. The ultimate foundation of business skills starts with many small ideas like the ones listed below. The real learning lies in doing things that require hard work, courage, and bravery. An example would be looking someone in the eye and asking them to write you a check or send payment of $495 for your services.

The Format for Each Idea

Obviously, every business idea here won't be perfectly suited for you. The point isn't to get overwhelmed or bogged down thinking you have to test out all 100 ideas. Rather, the idea is to read the list of 100 ideas at your leisure. Along the way, there might be something that strikes your fancy. An idea might jump out at you because your life experiences or existing skills have uniquely positioned you to get started. As a rule of thumb, business ideas where we can figure out the next step or action item to get started are the ones we are well suited to explore.

The more we take action, run experiments, and start side businesses, the more we'll learn what those next steps look like. After enough practice, it becomes second nature to identify the series of steps required to turn ideas into a cash generating business.

This list of 100 business ideas is meant to be a healthy snack. Eat them up and enjoy, but they purposefully don't cover every detail or intricacy of the business. They are meant to be creative fuel well suited for you to use wherever you are at. As you read them, and an idea jumps out at you, here are some questions you may want to ask yourself:

The Idea

- Is this a good fit for me?
- If so, why is it?
- Do I have a specific skill set or knowledge base that will give me the upper hand?
- Does it excite me?
- Can I think of the next step to take to get started?

As a rule of thumb, if you can take the next step to get started, this is a great sign that the business idea is perfectly suited to you, your network, and current business acumen. Now let's jump into the business ideas!

– 2 –

Technology and Technical Services

Media and Advertising Agency

Find out how a business is currently advertising and then begin exploring new advertising techniques, platforms, or distribution channels that might be useful to them. We can either teach them how to use this new tool or offer to buy advertisements for them through this new channel.

There is no better time to start a media or advertising buying agency that produces results. If you can buy ads for clients and demonstrate a positive return on investment, your skills will always be in demand. This is a type of business that you can understand by just figuring out a new advertising product on a social network. For instance, a new technical advertising product such as Facebook Dark Posts is a great place to start learning about an advertising product that your potential clients are most likely not using.

Or, you could learn a simple technical advertising tool like retargeting display advertisements. The major social networks will always have new advertising products which businesses are too busy to learn. That's where your media or advertising agency comes in. Whether it's Facebook,

Google, LinkedIn, Twitter, Amazon, or Podcasts, there is an opportunity to teach others how to advertise on these channels. These ever-changing platforms provide constant opportunity to add value to many businesses, and teach them the new advertising methods.

The future of advertising is increasingly technical, fragmented, social, quantifiable and mobile. If you begin now by learning a single product like Facebook Dark Posts, you can then learn what type of businesses could benefit from them. From there you can contact these businesses and offer your services. You might have to offer your services for a portion of the return on investment. (i.e. "I estimate that I can bring in $300 worth of business for you. I see that your margins are around 40%. What if I get 20% of that?") This quick example is a great way to figure out the upside and ensure a win-win for both parties. Not only is this is a low risk and low friction way to convince businesses to work with you in the beginning, but it also provides a great incentive to do an amazing job! By starting with a single technical advertising product, you can then begin to branch out and learn other social network's advertising products. This will ensure that you always have clients, as the markets will always be changing.

There are millions of people and businesses in our world who need someone to help them advertise on social media. Many of these businesses and people don't have time to understand or learn these new platforms and advertising products themselves. There is a huge business opportunity for any media/advertising agency that can advertise for a business and achieve measurable results with the latest advertising products.

This type of media purchasing is the future of advertising. The old days of hiring a PR firm and never getting any metrics, deliverables, or a return on your investment are over. When you buy ads or media you either see results or you don't. If you can learn this skill, teach it and consult with clients who need your expertise in purchasing new media, you have the start of a great business on your hands. Services will always be in demand for those who can learn how to use the latest advertising products on the latest social media platforms while delivering clients a measurable return on investment.

Mobile Agency

Many companies are ill prepared for the mobile smartphone revolution. Their websites, apps, or services are built for larger screen sizes. These millions of businesses desperately need mobile optimized or responsive websites. While customers are increasingly using their smartphones to access online services, websites are slow to adapt due to the smartphones broad array of operating systems and screen sizes. This points to a large opportunity for starting a business which builds responsive websites, mobile apps, or other software that is optimized for smartphones.*

It's estimated that there are 2 billion people who use the Internet regularly. The majority of those users (around 66%) are using smartphones, not traditional desktops or laptops. By 2020, it is projected that the number of people using smartphones will double to 4 billion people!

There has never been a better time to help small and medium size businesses become optimized for the coming wave of mobile smartphone users. For anyone interested in starting a business like this, there are hundreds of different avenues where this can be expanded. You could even get started by setting up simple template responsive (mobile ready) websites for people who are using existing infrastructures like Wordpress, Squarespace, or Shopify. As part of your services, you can teach your clients how to use those various platforms, or even charge them a monthly fee to maintain the technology you provide.

Responsive websites are those which adjust themselves to fit any screen size and look especially great on smartphones of all sizes.

Data Agency

The rate at which online users are generating data that's being collected is enormous. A thriving industry of today and the future is data science, which seeks to collect, measure and discover just what to do with this data. For those who learn data science, you can easily start a business that works with companies of all sizes to help them understand and utilize large datasets.

In 2013, we collectively generated around 4 zettabytes of data. By 2014, this number is projected to double. It's estimated that by 2020, smartphones, sensors, and the "Internet of things" will generate 44 zettabytes (that's 44 trillion gigabytes) of data.

Businesses and governments will increasingly pay money to the individuals or agencies which help them collect, filter, analyze, and capitalize on all this data. There are thousands of business opportunities in the field of data science. Whether you get started by learning Excel, R Studio, or even jump straight into JavaScript and Hadoop, there are thousands of business opportunities available for those who want them. Whether you want to start a freelancing or agency data science business, there will soon be 44 zettabytes of data waiting to be put to work.

Smart Homes Agency

"The internet of things" is a nickname given to the fact that the Internet is embedding itself in physical objects, connecting them in a way that has historically never been possible. Whether it's light switches, door locks, security systems, refrigerators, thermostats, watches, or cars, they're all becoming connected to the Internet. Software, sensors, and electronics are being placed into these products to transfer data to either the operator, other connected devices, or the manufacturer. As services like wink.com launch, they are catering (mainly) to early adopters. Wink's entire business model is built around helping those with the money, but not the time, to get a smartphone set up. Borrowing from Wink's idea, creating and setting up smart homes for individuals is only a service that will have increasing demand in the near future. There are a number of applications, smart technology and appliances which can be installed, linked, taught, and set up for homeowners, businesses, and governments.

Just some of the things you can install to create smart homes include door locks, thermostats, lights, speakers, shopping, and security systems. After getting everything set up, teach your customers how they can best use and utilize everything from their smartphone right away.

This type of agency and service will be increasingly in demand both now and in the future. People want efficiency and smart homes, but they're busy. The early adopters who can afford this now are happy to pay an expert to optimize their home for them. If you can set everything up and teach them to use their new smart home, this idea and business has big potential.

All the manufacturers of smart products such as thermostats, door locks, lights, speakers and tech equipment will likely offer you a partnership or wholesale deal on their products. These manufacturers want their products installed and used, not just purchased. These manufacturers know that laziness is the biggest hurdle to having their products used. Combat laziness with your smart home agency.

There are tons of ways to get started, but I would get started by catering to high net worth individuals only. Setting up "smart" homes could come at several price points from $1,000, $5,000 to $10,000 or more; this is a business idea ready to be started today.

RPAS and UAV Agency

"We're going to look outside in 10 years and the air is going to be thick with drones." –Marc Andreessen

The global demand for drones, UAVs (Unmanned Ariel Vehicles), or RPAS (Remote Piloted Aerial Systems) is growing geometrically. As RPAS improve, the demand for the services, technology and software that will give them the greatest utility is also growing. There will continue to be an increasing demand for experts in RPAS technology, hardware, software, services and legal strategies. The RPAS industry is poised for exponential growth.

It's estimated that in 2015 the RPAS industry hovers around $11.5 billion annually and could grow to over $140 billion in ten years.

RPAS experts in hardware, software, piloting, filming, data collection, computer science and deep learning are in demand.

There will be businesses that spring up within the RPAS community including new robotic attachments, apps with modified sensors, custom built UAVs, and software and hardware to power them. All these opportunities are ripe to be developed and turned into a thriving, forward-looking business.

Piloting and shooting high-quality video footage from RPAS' can open the door to a slew of business opportunities. Here are just a few businesses which will need RPAS video services: cruise lines, residential realtors, bars, clubs, content creators of all types, cinemas, commercial real estate, government, townships, farmers, hotels, retreats, national parks, marinas, ski resorts, and the list goes on!

Every travel and vacation destination, every event that is held outside – everything from craft fairs to Tough Mudder style events will begin utilizing RPAS. There is a business ready to be started today, even if it's starting as simple as creating the best local UAV filming agency. There are dollars willing to be spent on this as we speak, and from there your business can branch out into every other application. RPAS will fill the skies of the future. Whether you start your own business around them or join a business that is on the cutting edge of developing software and artificial intelligence for drones (Airwave and Skydio), RPAS' will be a business foundation for a long time to come.

Robotics and RPAS Security

The need for businesses which will ensure physical security is growing. As costs to begin and implement security businesses decrease, robotics and RPAS security will take precedence over traditional human-run models. A single security person can't cover many large facilities and spatial areas. But if that person has access to several robots or drones that can cover the entire area, they can use them to better secure any premises. Businesses will always need security and surveillance at reasonable prices. Chances are many businesses already have security providers they're happy with, but there are many opportunities to start a business that provides security by utilizing robotics and RPAS.

Whether you start a business that replaces their physical personnel and workforce, or you offer robotics and RPAS systems to enhance their existing security forces, the time to start a business in these areas is now. A single contract from a large corporation could launch a successful RPAS and robotics security agency. Eventually, this could expand to wider, more comprehensive security services via robotics, RPAS, with either AI (artificial intelligence) or remote-controlled vision systems. Businesses can leverage technology to replace the costs of a traditional security workforce with an indefatigable technological force.

Political Reform via Technology

Politics is one field in woeful need of reform. Did you know many politicians still rely on call centers to spread their messages? These political candidates and organizations are in desperate need of businesses which can help them use today's technology. Politicians desperately need to be introduced to the 21st century. If you understand technology, marketing, social media, data, design or coding, every single political campaign needs to hire you (or a business you start that offers those services).

Shrink Digital Footprints

There are many businesses that get their start by managing or shrinking people's online digital footprint. There is a great business opportunity always waiting for anyone with the ability to strategically and effectively help other people shrink their digital footprint.

Small and medium size businesses will pay a consultant plenty of money to teach them how and why they can use tools like DuckDuckGo, LifeLock, CyberDust, Expire, or any number of other services to better cap their liability. As privacy is becoming increasingly difficult, shrinking our digital footprints will be a field that continues to grow in the future. There is also a business, product or book waiting to be created to teach individuals how they can protect their online identity or shrink their digital footprint.

Video Agency

More videos are being uploaded to the Internet than ever before. The problem is many of their creators need help creating, editing, producing and publishing them. Many businesses, governments, and non-profits don't know where to begin. By starting a video agency, you can help them create videos to market their services, attract talented employees, and generally help them earn more business with high quality videos.

After you learn video production with your smartphone or Adobe Creative cloud, there are many people waiting to pay you for your services. There are even online platforms that already exist where people post the job they need done, and you can bid on it. Before bidding on a project, make sure to have a mini portfolio on your profile to showcase your amazing work.

Starting a video agency or consultancy is as simple as learning how to edit and produce videos, finding a company that needs videos, and helping them create great videos which will earn them more business. This type of video agency could offer consulting, video production, editing, or provide a variety of video content creation services. And who's to say you can't blend your drone agency with video recording and editing skills to become a highly sought after video agency!

Graphical Content Creation

Towards the end of our video agency business example, we suggested that ultimately, that business could develop into a digital content creation company. Great digital content is becoming increasingly in demand. Businesses can't just advertise; they need to create content which gains attention, and then put it in front of their ideal customers using social media. Those who understand how to create eye-catching content and distribute it using social media channels already has a significant business opportunity in their hands.

You can start a digital content creation agency by starting in one niche, such as our previous example of video. Or, you could begin by mastering a software service like Canva. With Canva, you can easily create and share graphics, infographics, Twitter cards, content for Facebook dark posts, and beautiful graphical lists for Pinterest. Having a creative eye, and the ability to beautify content is always a skill that is in high demand.

Technical Services

The bright side of learning technical skills is that most people won't do it. It takes too much time and effort, or they convince themselves that they are "just technologically challenged."

If you are brave and stubborn enough to learn technical skills, you're likely always one step away from growing a business around those skills. There always seems to be a demand for people who can learn new technological skills such as design or coding. The exciting part about learning and getting paid for your technical skills is that it's the foundation of a service-based business. The amazing part about solid technical service based businesses is that they can be productized over time. In other words, the consulting or services you offer can be automated by using technology. An example of this would be Basecamp. They started as a web design company and then created a web app, Basecamp, which would help them manage their internal consulting, teams, and projects. The web app they built to solve an internal problem was something they could also offer their customers. Now, instead of just trading their time for dollars, they built a service that could be sold independently of their time.

When you're able to productize your service offerings, you can remove yourself from having to repetitiously perform certain tasks. When you offer your personal services or physically dependent expertise, you're trading your time for money. When you trade a product for money, now you're selling your time in a much more effective (and scalable) way.

Automation and Time Provider

Most people don't use technology to their advantage. Did you know you can link your social media accounts, email, and virtually every web app there is? That's right. For example, let's say that you have a weekly newsletter, or a product that you sell online. When someone signs up for your email newsletter or buys a product of yours, you can have an automatic email sent to one of your employees that reminds them to reach out and thank the individual who signed up. This can happen anytime during the day, without you even thinking about it! This email service functionality called an autoresponder is well known, but there are many follow up automated services you can add. For instance, you can automate everything from scheduling your blog posts to go out at predetermined times, to sending out your to-do items to your employee's phones as soon as you right them. Many people understand that the ability to link apps and services together online exist, but few businesses understand this. This business idea would be starting a business or consulting service that provides this for already established businesses. This business model is one of helping people automate things, and selling them back time. The popularity of services and companies like Uber, and grocery delivery services all prove that people love buying time and convenience. There are many companies both large and small that need help automating their repetitive tasks by using automation services like IFTTT or Zapier.

Once you become proficient using either one of these services, you'll discover that there are thousands of ways you can link apps together so they function in a smart fashion. As social media platforms expand, linking accounts and automating actions is necessary to build a growing presence online.

Business Validation

Start a business that validates other business ideas for a fee. Many people don't realize there is a ton of research that goes into formulating a great business idea and then testing it out. If you're willing to start several businesses, you'll rapidly learn that searching Google Trends, keyword searches, App Store search results, Amazon searchers, Patents, Trademarks, economic data, willingness to pay, Facebook ads, and a thousand more variables is important if you want to seriously test a business idea before you jump all the way in. Consider offering a service where you validate business ideas for other people.

Marketplace

Create an advertising network or marketplace. Did you know a skilled developer can build an entirely functional marketplace like Fiverr or AirBnb over the weekend? They can; it's of course more basic, but you get the idea. Come up with an idea that will attract both buyers and sellers, and then offer a novel way to bring them together by providing information and peer vetting that will establish trust on the platform. While creating great marketplaces isn't easy, they are amazing businesses when executed well.

Technical Manufacturing

Technical manufacturing is a field poised to explode. They can't find enough skilled applicants, workers or executives in many roles ranging from repair to actual engineering. Learn the industry and join a program like GE's GetSkillstoWork, and start your own business helping this exploding industry. Bonus points for helping them transition into 3D printing.

Applied Exercise and Experiments

Now's the time to take a break, synthesize what we've covered, and blend it with your experiences and expertise! Our goal with the exercise below is to make the section above work for you.

Before we move on to the next section, pat yourself on the back. Few people have the ability to think about multiple ideas at once. Even fewer have enough faith to consider starting a business or a side income stream. So few people achieve financial security because they never develop multiple income streams. Now is the time to let your subconscious go to work and mix the ideas we just covered with your experience, expertise, and knowledge.

Here are a couple questions for you to consider:
- Does any of the ideas listed above blend uniquely with your existing skill set?
- Can you blend any of the ideas together? For example, did you like the ideas mentioned about RPAS services that you can blend with the health care idea? Could you combine the two ideas and offer aerial RPAS footage for medical clients? This example is incredibly niche, but it's just an illustration of how layering and blending ideas together might yield a

business perfectly suited for your skills, with minimal competition.

- ◆ Or, how about blending some of these pieces with any existing ideas that you already have?
- ◆ Were any brand new ideas sparked? If so, write them down quickly!
- ◆ If a particular idea jumped out at you above, what single step could you take today to get started?

That wraps up our applied exercise! If you've completed the exercise, over the course of the next few days, your subconscious mind might start serving up a variety of new ideas. Or, you might stumble on the perfect next step to get started on one of the ideas we've previously covered. Whenever you have those new ideas or sparks of inspiration, don't be afraid to get started immediately!

- 3 -

Creatives, Artists, Inspirational Leaders

B.E.D.S

There are only four professions, or core skills and job functions, in the new economy. Although the types of different jobs will be broad, every job falls under four main "skill" areas. The acronym I use to segment and break down the type of jobs which can be turned into businesses, or which will be in high demand by other businesses, is BEDS:

Business Developers: sales, growth, strategy, marketing, social media content, full-stack marketing, general leadership, storytellers, authors, artists, etc. Business developers include artists who want to begin quantifying the value they deliver to others. In order to survive in this transitional period where technology causes everything to fragment, art is needed in business as much as business is needed in art. As new media emerges in a fragmented fashion, designers and artists must master technology and apply basic business principals to the fruits of their design labors if they want access to the upside from their work.

Engineers: mechanical engineers, machinists, tradesmen, developers, front-end, back-end, full-stack, and the whole makers movement.

Designers: UX/UI, HTML/CSS, Photoshop CS, social media content, wireframes, sketching, rapid prototyping, 3D printing. This also includes anyone who creates art.

Scientists: data science, traditional scientists, statisticians, computer scientists, biologists, and medicinal researchers. These professions require a mastery of manipulating, understanding, and making prescriptions based on huge sets of data. Real scientists will be anti-fundamentalists.

If you can master the skills that fall under any of these categories, you will have the opportunity to start a profitable business.

Storytelling

Write fiction on Amazon if you're creative. You can publish your fiction using KDP Select and Kindle Unlimited. Or you can upload and distribute it using Smashwords, which publishes it to iTunes, Kobo and other retailers. If you love to write, there has never been a better time to do so and get paid. Writing them is only half the battle; finding distribution, exposure, marketing, and selling are additional challenges. The good news for writers is that if you create something people love, social media is now ripe for your message to be spread.

The two best professionals to learn from who self-publish their work profitably are James Altucher and Hugh Howey. Learn from James if you want to publish non-fiction. Learn from Hugh if you want to publish fiction. Or learn from both. If you can write and tell stories that people like, now is an amazing time to capitalize on this skill.

Expert in New Technologies

Niche down and become an expert on a specific topic that not many people know about. For instance, Bitcoin and Blockchain are new technologies that very few people understand.

Now is the time to become a subject matter expert. If you look at the broader opportunity, the entire finance industry is being transformed by technology. Bitcoin and Blockchain are two examples of financial technologies that are the future of that industry. There are many instances like this in every industry where emerging technologies are not properly understood or valued by the marketplace. Becoming an expert might begin by getting to know what companies are innovating in the space. From there, figure out what skills they need, and see how you can go about learning that technology. As a side note, when we refer to "technology" throughout this book, it's important to define the word. Technology is purely the ability to do more, with less. Technology by itself is neither good, nor bad. It is our vision, intentions and how we wield the technology that determines what it produces.

Along the path of learning new technology, there are ways to speed up your knowledge accumulation. You could: start or join a local meet-up that discusses that technology, write for an online news site about the technology, join a LinkedIn group, start a Medium collection, or research the topic and publish that research as several small, non-fiction eBooks or articles. You could even go online, read dozens of new technology product reviews, find where the new technology is lacking, and then hypothesize about how to fix the shortcomings. Prepare your ideas for how to make the technology better into a report/article, or send it to the company that creates it. This is how the best jobs, writing spots, and consulting gigs are sparked. They aren't pre-existing; they need you to create them!

Once you learn enough about whichever new technologies you studied, keep compounding your learning until it becomes clear that you know enough to provide value to others. Along the way, make sure to share your findings and learning. Write about it, talk about it, share your findings, and keep working until you find yourself an expert on the cutting edge of technologies that are building or reshaping industries. Along that path, there will be many opportunities to start a business. Specific business ideas here could include discovering that there is demand for a specific newsletter that subscribers will pay to receive. Or, why not get together with a group of friends to build software that the market needs! The opportunities are endless.

Whether you begin learning about Bitcoin or RPAS systems, more experts and leaders are needed in these emerging technologies.

Expert in Your "Superpower"

What have you already spent more time learning than anyone else? Is there a field, pursuit, hobby, or something that comes naturally to you? Is there something you do naturally that amazes others, and doesn't feel like work? So often, we are oblivious to our own unique skills and talents that would be the perfect starting point for a business or income stream. What can you do that looks like a "superpower" to others but comes naturally to you? This is often the best place to start a business. If you have ideas about what this is, write them down! How can you sell or offer your expertise to others? If you don't know what your superpowers are, ask those closest to you. Find out what they see in you that you might not even realize. If you don't have anyone close to you, or honest enough, stop reading this book and go find someone! But joking aside, you might already be closer to having a superpower than you know, which is the perfect starting point for a great business.

Some other questions you can ask to help turn your superpower into a business include:

◆ What are you already spending most of your time learning and doing? Pay special attention to your free time, or what you are thinking about while you are on the job. Are you constantly compiling healthy recipes to cook, but can't seem to organize them the way you want? Do you love to organize day trips when your friends come to visit your town or city? Or maybe you are detail oriented, and constantly find yourself perfecting electronic documents from other people. Small things like this could turn into great businesses if one is willing to step back and examine their daily actions to the fullest.

◆ Is there an area where you're an expert that others are not? If you zeroed in on that area and doubled down your efforts, how good could you become? Top 5%? Top 1% or .001%?

◆ What do you do better than anyone else that doesn't feel like work to you, but everyone else complains about? If you can take away their complaints with either your service or expertise, you're well on your way to starting a business around your skills!

When your personal knowledge and skills can deliver value and save others time and heartache, or increase a business' or individual's earnings, you have a business on your hands.

You can offer your services to others as coaching, work for hire, consulting, or build a product around what you love to do (you might love it, but if other people hate it, they'll pay you to remove that discomfort!).

The greatest test of whether or not you're ready to be hired for your skills or expertise is: will family or friends hire you, and will they recommend your (paid) services to someone else they know. If you can pass this test, then full speed ahead and build your business! Contrary to popular belief, many times it's actually harder to get your family to buy what you're selling, and if you can pass that test, you're in great shape. However, one catch is that you don't want to pick the easiest, most supportive family member to sell to. If you know your mom will buy a rock out of her own backyard from you, then your mom cannot be your test!

Some examples of where you might have a personal superpower that allows you to start a business:

- Relationships coach (you have a great relationship that other people aspire to find)
- Health or nutrition coach (you have a great body, fitness routine, and lifestyle that others desire)
- Fiduciary (you have your finances, real estate, multiple income streams, retirement savings perfected. Or, you are generally in an enviable financial position that you've created through hard work)
- Mobile advertising app installs expert
- Tutor for any standardized test or certification

Non-Fiction Writing

Write non-fiction guides on Amazon to present solutions to people's problems. Study commonly asked questions on Quora to get an idea of what problems you can solve. You can also study the "most helpful" three-star reviews of existing non-fiction books. Those three-star reviews will likely illuminate what people were hoping to learn from a book, but didn't. You can create a better solution to their challenges and present it. You could publish your non-fiction writing under a pen name if you're worried about how your writing will be perceived. You could even start by offering summaries of other business books, write how-to articles, or offer stories to others of how you solved personal challenges. Thanks to KDP and Kindle Unlimited, it's never been easier to publish and get distribution for non-fiction that aims to teach and solve problems.

Writing or Content Company

Start a writing and content company. You can start the business by writing or producing content for blogs. Then you can outsource the writing aspect of the business, and just edit the content that you outsourced. Top __ lists are dead simple. Read James Altucher's <u>30 Tips for Better Writing</u> and you'll be off to the races. Find a few people or content sites that will pay you for what you write. Start off writing for those with a high ability to pay, and who will greatly benefit if you help them make just a single extra sale. Create a profile or website for yourself and services, and make sure to list any writing projects you have complete. A sample of work is key to gaining clients! You can eventually build this into an agency. Maybe a personal brand will work initially to find clients, or maybe the appearance of an agency allows you to find more business. After you get started with a few paying customers, you can create profiles for your services on many existing sites and marketplaces like oDesk, Fiverr, Contently, or Thumbtack.

All these profiles can be turned into well-oiled machines that bring your business a stream of clients. After you master the art of writing articles that help other businesses, you can expand into offering other forms of content creation (as your margins allow). This small start has the potential to turn into an agency, or you may even stumble onto an idea that allows you to productize your service. An example of productizing your service would be offering to create a certain amount of content a month for a business, charging either a set price or monthly subscription plan.

Audio Narrator

If you have a great speaking voice, now is the perfect time to become an Audible narrator. I didn't realize just how much they made for a single book until I hired one! Their services are in increasing demand, and if you have the time, the voice, and a microphone you'll want to consider recording audiobooks. Voiceover work is easy to do just about anywhere, and in only several months you can become proficient at recording, editing, and producing audiobooks or various other forms of narration services. With the need for this service exploding, you'd think there would be a million high-quality audio narrators. But surprisingly, there aren't that many high quality firms or amazing narrators. You can start this business on many different existing platforms like Fiverr, oDesk, and Audible (ACX).

Artist in Residence

Consider starting a business as an Artist in Residence. What does this mean? It simply means you become an "idea sitter." There are businesses right now, especially in technology, which will pay you to generate great ideas for them. They might call these consultant spots by different terms, or maybe you've heard them referred to as "creative director" roles. But if you can generate a steady stream of great ideas, eventually you'll find somebody who will want to pay, partner, or hire you to generate more.

Platforms like Quirky already allow creative's to submit ideas for products. The community votes on the ideas, and the best ones are turned into real products. The creators/inventors get a percentage of all sales. The Quirky platform, and the idle cash in the bank and on balance sheets of many companies is evidence that there is a shortage of good ideas about what to produce.

Stakes and Incentives as a Service

Why do we know what we should do, but just don't do it? Behavioral psychologists who study this phenomenon have coined several terms that help us understand it. These researchers have found that we act appropriately and achieve results when we have proper stakes and incentives surrounding our goals. That is to say, when we have the proper cultural, social, and financial incentives and stakes we can't help but achieve what we want. Many people are always looking for an "accountability buddy", but they never dive into the research behind stakes and incentives. If you explore the research around stakes and incentives, you'll discover that you can offer it as a service to others who are struggling to achieve what they want.

Text Coach

In the spirit of the previous business idea of accountability as a service, one of the fastest growing career fields is coaching. It's a bit like consulting, but it's perfectly suited for those individuals who are empathetic and patient, and who genuinely want others to do their best. You can sign up to be a Coach at sites like Coach.me (formerly known as Lift).

Relationships Coach

There is another area where coaching, teaching, incentives, and stakes are greatly needed. It's in relationships. The problem is that many people are too embarrassed to seek help for their relationships. If you offer relationship training, consider offering your services over the phone and through text messages. This is a business opportunity that is currently being underutilized.

New Media Agent

Become an agent for new media stars. Whether it's on YouTube, Vine, Snapchat or anywhere else, there are thousands of micro-celebrities. Some of them will be the next superstars. Agents typically make 15% of deals when they sell or book one of their clients. Learn about the field and help these micro-celebrities land advertisements, endorsement deals, product affiliate deals, or even sell a show pilot featuring several of them.

Podcast Network

Create a podcast or media network. Many people are starting podcasts now, but few of them are going about it in efficient ways. If you're skilled with audio or production, you can help great personalities get on air as podcasters on your network.

Artist

This business idea for creating and selling art might be obvious to you. But what might not be obvious are the new distribution channels that are opening up for artists. If you create art such as paintings, drawings, and other physical products, there are now services like Printful that can take care of all the creation, printing, and fulfillment of your orders. Massive retailers like Amazon have just opened up their art store, and the opportunity to be one of the first artists with your paintings for sale on an E-Commerce giant like Amazon is unprecedented.

Health Results Specialist

If you're into health and fitness and understand stakes and incentives, you should consider creating a business around personal training that actually works! Think about all the people who start eating healthy and getting in shape, but then quit. They do this because they don't have the right stakes and incentives set up. This is where a personal trainer that gets results comes in! If you're an expert in health and fitness, offer Personal Training that is guaranteed to work as long as clients do: a, b, and c. You can set up the right stakes, incentives, and milestones, and you'll be well on your way to achieving results and creating happy clients for life.

- 4 -

Sales

Sales Consultant

We're entering a golden age for those who can help others sell online. Just about everyone is one step away from starting a business as a sales consultant, affiliate, or contractor who helps existing businesses sell more things. All it takes is analyzing what you already purchase and what products or services you're most passionate about, and then discovering how you can assist in selling them. This is a business that can evolve from just getting an affiliate account and selling online or in person for a local business.

Pick out a product that you either use or you're in awe of. Reach out to the business that creates it and find out how you can help them sell it. You could offer your services at first as a consultant to the company, or as a contractor. By choosing a specific "Industry A" and "Product A", you could form a business that helps train anyone in *Industry A* sell more of *Product A*.

This business could evolve quickly into aligning yourself with startups that need excellent salespeople. Once you become a master of sales and great at using technology to sell, you can create an account on a platform like AngelList. There, you'll find startups creating interesting hardware and software which are in desperate need of skilled salespeople and sales consultants.

Tradesy

Sell your unused clothing (or your spouse's) on Tradesy.com. Set up a consignment shop and sell clothes or other goods online. Practice selling popular apparel on eBay or Amazon. Focus on making a small margin at first, and gradually increase it. In the process, you might discover a particular product, piece of fashion, or collectible which has a margin high enough where you can start a business through buying and selling it.

Crafts

Set up an Etsy store to sell your crafts or artisanal creations. If you don't make crafts, you can set up stores for those in your area who do. Or find amazing products being created by the best artisans in a spatial area. You could curate them and create an online store for a group which otherwise wouldn't have one. Or you could offer a monthly market basket of crafts from local artisans. The monthly box subscription business is booming right now, whether it's a box full of healthy snacks or dog treats. Creating a monthly box full of local artisan gifts would do extremely well within this business model. Especially if each month the box was a different "local flavor", containing local artisan products from different cities around the country.

Simplify as a Service

Simplify and declutter your life. Then help others do the same. Junk collecting is a billion dollar industry. Decluttering and simplification as a service is something many Americans would happily pay for. Sell every single extra "thing" in your life that you don't use on eBay and Craigslist today. Why? You'll gain practice in the art of selling. You'll improve your advertising, sales and negotiation skills through selling goods. In the process, you'll declutter your house and life, which can provide you with a positive mental boost.

The quicker and more efficient you become better at writing catchy ads and selling, the better you'll be as an entrepreneur. One of the ways to become entrepreneurial is to sell something – anything – as quickly as possible. The second way is through decreasing the clutter or extraneous stuff in your life whenever possible. You can expand this service into a business and help others sell all the extra things they no longer want.

Flipping

Flipping (insert decently priced electronic or mechanical tool here). Take cars for an example. Can you clean up and fix cars? If you can do the work necessary to clean or fix older or broken cars, perhaps buying and selling them is a great fit for you. The lifespan of cars (and many other electronics or mechanical tool out there) is rapidly increasing. The influx of 68 million immigrants to the U.S. between now and 2050 means there are millions of people who need low-cost transportation, electronics, and tools. This is a great near-term start to begin making cash if you're mechanically inclined. If your prospective buyers don't have enough cash to pay you, simply negotiate a deal with a local financing company or bank. You refer the customer who wants to buy what you're offering to them. If the margin is slim on the products you're flipping, you can still make money for sending the financing company the customer lead. Considering the fact that new banking customers are worth thousands to tens of thousands of dollars to banks, a lead generation service for banks could be a business in and of itself.

Food Truck

Why take the risk of starting a restaurant when you can start with a food truck?

In cities all over the country, food trucks are springing up everywhere. They require a significantly lower startup cost than any restaurant with a physical location. Find a local food truck that is crushing it and figure out what they're doing right, or even go work for them for a while. From there you can partner with a food truck business that is already working well, or you can launch your own food truck that specializes in something specific such as coffee and bagels.

A food truck is a small, lower risk bet when compared to a restaurant. A great resource for learning how to start a food truck business is http://foodtruckr.com

- 5 -

E-Commerce

Online School or University

Create your own online school with Fedora. This web-app and hosting service for online courses and schools is a turnkey solution to teaching classes online. You can create classes or partner with others who have their own courses. You could start by partnering with a business that needs a very specific type of trained employee. Create a training program that the business approves of, offer it as a course to prospective applicants via Fedora,[1] and help your partner business by sending them trained workers. The business model can net a small amount up front for teaching people skills, as well as making money for referring highly trained candidates to your business partner.

E-Commerce Store

Open an E-Commerce Store. Want to sell t-shirts, posters or swag? Create a store with merchandise that people want to wear, simply by slapping a design, logo, saying, or catchy cartoon on a shirt. Start a store using a turnkey commerce solution like Shopify. Link Shopify to fulfillment services which take care of all the printing costs, shipping, and fulfillment for you in exchange for a cut of your sales. You can set all this up and have a beautifully designed store via Shopify linked with Printful (which makes, prints, and fulfills orders for physical goods). You can set up a Shopify site in a few minutes with a couple clicks. After that, Printful has one-click integration. Now, when customers browse your website, they can click "order" for a shirt, mug, or poster. Shopify takes care of the payment and Printful takes care of the fulfillment.

Drop Shipping

In the previous example, we talked about how you can sell posters or swag with Shopify and Printful. Printful takes care of creating the item and sending it for you. This is also known as "drop shipping".

You don't have to sell just swag via drop shipping. Many companies offer drop shipping options for their products. This means you can have an online store which sells products for others. Customers order through your site and the drop shipping company takes care of sending them their orders.

This business idea simply involves setting up an e-commerce website, and then finding a database of other people's products to sell. Thousands of products are available through businesses who want to partner with others to expand their distribution. You can sell these products through your online store and another company handles fulfillment. The margins might be small at first, but you can make up for this in volume. You can also sell these products while utilizing your own brand through sites like Amazon.

– 6 –

Platform and Marketplace Arbitrage

The Transporter

At the time of this writing, Uber had been recently valued at over $40 billion! Many Uber drivers make over $200 a day, and Uber isn't the only option for becoming a transporter.

Whether it's Uber, Lyft, or Leap Transit, these companies need high-quality drivers. They have a high willingness to pay for great work and you can start your own transporting service in less than a month. Simply log onto to their platforms, sign up, and start driving. There will be competition if you're in a big city, but if you're in a smaller city you could be the first mover.

Pet Services as a Service

People love their pets. There will always be a demand for loving pet caretakers and providers. Whether you train, walk, feed, groom, or just pet sit, you can start making money by taking care of pets today.

You can easily find clients by signing up as a caretaker on sites like DogVacay.com, or you can reach out to friends who have pets.

There is an opportunity to niche your services down and become an expert by working with specific exotic pets or breeds. There are people out there ready to pay for a pet sitter for their animals throughout the day. If you love animals, you can start a business that takes care of them!

Underutilized Asset Liquidation

This $20 fancy phrase simply means selling or renting time with an asset that other people want. Maybe you have a top tier camera that photographers would want to rent for a day. Maybe you have an amazing drone that people would pay you money to test fly or rent for an event.

Consider that many Americans have homes and cars that go largely unused. There is a great local business opportunity ready for anyone who can help others get cash for their unused goods. Whether that is helping someone else rent their house through AirBnB, or helping them rent their car through RelayRides, if you help others make money, you can make money.

People use the term "sharing economy" sometimes to describe this buying, selling, and renting of durable goods. But it's not really sharing; it's getting more use out of valuable things. In the past, this was very difficult, but now technology is making this easier than ever.

A business is ready to be started by helping others tap the liquidity in their underutilized assets. Whether it's getting them setup on AirBnb or RelayRides, the opportunity is there to help bring them value.

– 7 –

Events and Activities

Events Intro

Traditional retail is dying. E-commerce and expedited shipping are exploding in popularity and demand. The retail stores that survive over the long term will gradually turn into destinations which host a variety of events, or generally offer fun activities for the attendees.

If you look at many Whole Foods locations, they teach cooking and craft classes at their stores. If you look at Lululemon Athletica (premium athletic and yoga gear), you will see that many of their stores have yoga areas where they hold classes.

The business opportunity here is to help retail businesses transform into destinations for not just their goods, but for services, events, classes, and activities!

Alternative Education

There is an increasing demand for day care, charter schools, and private Montessori-style schools where top-notch teachers teach children relevant curriculum. Whether you start a business working for a school like this or start your own, the time is approaching where parents will not only demand high-quality care for their children, but they'll expect them to be taught in-demand skills as well.

Camp

Did you ever go to camp as a kid? Most people either had one of two experiences at after school programs or summer camps. We either loved it or we hated it. This points to a big business opportunity. Offer parents an amazing alternative to the terrible, or at best mediocre, existing camps in your area. Whether you begin by offering a single class, after school camp, or a camp which offers trips and traveling, parents are happy to pay good money to know their children are safe, learning rapidly, and building social skills with peers.

Performance Based Service (Antifragile Skill)

This class of service-based businesses include bartending, catering, babysitting, elder care, street performers (like jugglers, poets, artists) day laborers, home cleaning, and many others. These all seem simple, but they are what author and entrepreneur Nassim Taleb deems, "antifragile."

These skills will be in demand for much of the foreseeable future. Advances in technology or robotics are not happening quickly enough to immediately replace them. As a result, these performance-based skills are actually more secure than the average white-collar job. They are resilient to economic shocks or layoffs, and there are many people always willing to pay for these services.

We mentioned a few services above, but each of them is the possible start of a business. Depending on how you expand, service, and promote your work, your business will grow accordingly. There are so many performance-based skills in demand, whether it's photography, cooking, decorating, singing, comedy, or even juggling. Once you can entertain, delight, or help a small audience with your performance, you'll have the start of a real business on your hands.

If you perform with just a bit more energy and aptitude than the average person, you will begin building an antifragile skill that can provide a side stream of income, as opposed to corporate employee who (usually) only has one.

Wine Tasting

There is a great business opportunity in starting a wine of the month or wine tasting events. You can partner with local vineyards, restaurants, bars, or event venues to set up tasting events.

Find locations that have downtime or days of the month where they are not as busy. Offer to bring them customers in exchange for hosting your wine event. You could contact ten vineyards and get bottles of their wines to use as tasting samples. You can offer a special deal to those who attend and want to purchase wine. Along with selling the event tickets and selling wine from your partner vineyards, the restaurant you host it at could pay you for bringing in customers. You could potentially set up a deal with the restaurant where a certain percent of restaurant food sales for that day can be your commission.

Craft Beer Making and Tasting

Craft beer making and tasting is exploding in popularity! To start a business in this area, you can teach people how to make their own craft beer. Put up some flyers that say "FREE BEER" and include the event time and place. Or you can put up a sign that says "LEARN TO MAKE BEER" and "GET FREE BEER." Find a local brewery, bar, or venue you can partner with. If people don't want to pay for tickets, ask the venue or brewery if they'll pay you for bringing people in. If you can bring 100 people to a bar or venue on an off day or time, I strongly suspect they'll give you a nice cut of the proceeds.

Wine Bar or Craft Brew Pub

If you're into wine or beer, why not open up your own vineyard or craft brew pub? A craft brew pub or wine bar is a great business for many reasons. The number one reason is that people like to drink. The second reason is that there is a plethora of new local beers and wines that need to be curated by experts. Entrepreneur and investor Gary Vaynerchuk got his start by curating and selling wine at his family's liquor-turned-wine store. Whether you start a craft brew pub, wine bar, or vineyard, you can start by making or selling your own booze.

You can gain the operational knowledge needed to do this by working at an existing store, and then branching out and opening your own. Or you can find a few co-founders and start a place of your own. If you have a physical space such as a storefront, there are many income streams you can create by hosting events or renting out the bar and brew space.

One additional thought would be to try and put your own spin on the wine or beer that you make or sell. Are you able to make the wine/beer in a way that is very different than your competition? What are the trends swirling around the marketplace right now that may fit into your business?

Organic? Goes well with tofu or grass-fed beef? Smaller, eco-friendly containers? Whatever it is, try to fit your product into a market trend that other wine or beer companies are not currently capitalizing on.

Relationship Building Events

While dating apps abound, there are still many people who want to meet potential dates only in person. There is a business opportunity for relationship coaches or counselors who want to host relationship finding or coaching events. You can host a seminar where you introduce guys to women (or vice versa) and help them step up their relationship skills.

If you're a woman, you can host an event for guys where they can practice talking to women. If you're a guy, you can help women meet guys who aren't weirdos. Author and entrepreneur Michael Ellsberg was able to host (and monetize) "eye-gazing parties" where people met up and just stared at each other. There is no reason you can't host a meet-up, coaching, speed dating, or relationship seminar if you've built a great relationship of your own.

Offer people an opportunity to practice improving their speaking and relationship skills in a place where everyone around them is doing the same. This type of positive social pressure can help many of them overcome their relationship fears.

Forced Public Speaking

The number one fear people continually cite is public speaking. A great event business opportunity is to host a day, weekend, or even week-long event where you help people crush their fear of public speaking and improve at it.

So many people are terrified of speaking in public purely because they have not done it often enough to feel confident yet. Many people would love to overcome this fear, but don't know how. In our day-to-day lives, depending on our careers, we rarely have an opportunity to speak in public.

You can start a business by hosting an event that helps people learn to speak in public by speaking in front of the attendees of the event. Don't allow phones or pictures inside the event, in order to give people a comfortable and safe place to practice. This business idea could be extremely lucrative if executed well. You can create an event where you have a day of short structured talks where people get on stage and speak several times in front of the conference attendees. You could start off by having them walk on stage, introduce themselves, then walk off with everyone clapping. This builds up their confidence to get started. You can have all the attendees cycle onto the stage, and gradually increase the time that each of them speaks. Eventually, they won't even realize they've become comfortable speaking in front of a room filled with people! For an event idea like this, you only need 50 people paying $97 each to clear $5000 in revenue. In order to get better at public speaking, people need to have incentives and stakes, and this means building up a series of successful small "wins" by talking in front of a real audience. By coordinating an event like this, you can help most people overcome their number one fear in life.

Local Industry Event

You would think that by now, there wouldn't be any opportunity left in hosting amazing local meet-ups. But surprisingly, there are very few people who execute on this business model well. There is plenty of opportunity for those who learn how to host and throw amazing local networking events. You can get started by joining a group of local industry experts in a specific niche you're an expert in, or are just interested in learning more about. You can gather 20 local experts who want to get together to exchange business ideas and referrals.

Maybe you can start a book club specific to their business and industry. The idea is to find people who own businesses that could do more or better business if you helped them network at a great, uplifting event. Create and host that event for them.

Mastermind

A mastermind group is a group of individuals working together and meeting who help one another reach their goals. You can create a mastermind group of your own where you have skills, and where you can help the attendees accomplish specific goals.

To get started, you can begin gathering a group of people who are all working towards a similar goal. Maybe it's a business, lifestyle, or education ambition.

If you don't have a way to get the word out about your event, find somebody who does and split the ticket sales with them. Maybe you're getting your graduate degree. Find others nearby who are getting that same degree, and start meeting up to strategize together about the best ways you can accomplish your goals.

Break Into _____ Event

There is another business opportunity waiting for those who can help others learn technology, and then acquire jobs at technology companies.

A growing number of people want to learn how to become developers, programmers, designers, or just want to learn how to use new technology.

Many people want to become involved with startups but don't know how. You can start this business by learning a platform such as AngelList or searching the INC 500 and discovering the types of people that companies want to hire. They usually want to hire all technologically skilled employees!

Find out the exact specifications of who and what these companies need. From there, you could start by hosting an event for anyone who wants to learn those in-demand skills. You can partner with the companies who want to do the hiring, along with the companies that will do the training. As the event host, you can simply be the facilitator of that serendipity.

You could even start an event like this at a local

community college or university. If you find that many of the people signing up for your event don't have the basic credentials, you can offer them training through a separate event. To facilitate the training they might need, you can reach out to local training providers, developer boot camps, or IT training companies.

Partner and JV Events

There are, at any given time, thousands of businesses in your state that could be working together. They're busy keeping their own lights on, and don't know how they can partner. They won't know until you introduce them and provide them with an easy way to set up a partnership.

An example of starting a business by helping two businesses partner or collaborate for a joint venture could be promoting an up-and-coming company which is disrupting an industry. The up-and-coming company is most likely to be completely changing an industry or cutting out the middlemen. An example might be Redfin, which is disrupting real estate. There are many existing real estate agents who would be making a lot more money by working for them, but they simply don't know about the opportunity. Redfin and frustrated realtors are two groups that need to meet and partner together!

There are many frustrated realtors right now who need more business. By helping them understand how Redfin is changing their market, you're serving them. They might want to work for Redfin, or they'll realize how their industry is being transformed, or how they can become more skilled. You can host an event and offer the two entities (Company A and Person or Company B) training to help them better partner with each other. In the process, you'll likely stir up a business opportunity, a consulting offer, or maybe even a job offer to work with Redfin.

Another example might be hosting an event for college students or frustrated cab drivers who are interested in working nights and weekends at a great part-time to full-time job. Introduce them and train them in how they can drive for Lyft or Uber. Then help the best candidates and drivers acquire jobs at Lyft and Uber.

Keeping up with the most current companies or technologies is a full-time job. Helping others gain insight into the rapidly changing industries around them will always provide a great business opportunity.

Hobbyist Event

Turn your existing passions into profit. A great way to do this is by hosting a hobbyist-based event. You can find and use space for the event at places like your local WeWork, General Assembly, or whatever incubator or accelerator is near you.

Examine your own hobbies. Are there groups of people who want to meet to talk about them? Get them together.

You could purchase a few cheap drones/UAV's/RPAS's and host a hobbyist event around that technology. Or you could throw together a unique display of scrapbooks, and show your guests how to make the most creative scrapbook from materials they would not usually consider. The idea is to see if you can create an experience around that hobby which others will pay to attend. Or, you can start hosting a hobbyist event for which the businesses that create the technology used for your specific hobby will pay.

If you can create something good enough that those around you will buy (not just to be nice), you're well on your way to building the entrepreneurial muscle.

Multipurpose Event Space

Grab, rent, or buy a small space of your own and make it into a multi-purpose event space.

You could start a bar, breakfast, lunch, dinner, craft brewery, co-working space, wedding locale, etc. You can work at a popular event space in your area and then figure out how to help them expand, or start your own!

Multipurpose event spaces are a unique way to create a lower risk storefront by having multiple streams of income coming in from different groups of customers.

Personal Training for Large Groups

When done right, personal training for large groups of people will always be a viable business opportunity. Whether you're in the fitness arena, or you train job seekers on how to get set up and use LinkedIn, conducting training for large groups of people is a great business model.

If you're close to a metro area, you'll be able to easily sell and fill classes for 50 to 100 people at a time. You could host events that are single or even multi-day. An example might be in the fitness arena: you could sell a weekend training event where people get three personalized workouts along with extended yoga sessions over three days. You can get creative and blend classes together that nobody else offers. For instance, you can offer kettle-bell classes combined with yoga and pilates. Or you can offer strength training with a blend of sprints, shuttle runs, and barre classes. You can offer personal training or dance classes. The potential ideas are endless for hosting large group training, but if you can create fun classes and teach them en masse, you have a business on your hands. The personalized personal trainer only gets to work with one person at a time, whereas these types of events will allow you the latitude to work with hundreds of people at once. Now that's efficiency!

As the courses and events you offer become better, you can even film and sell these sessions online as you go, or broadcast them for free on YouTube. While doing this, make sure to advertise how to sign up or buy tickets for your in-person classes. As you progress, splice together different sections of your work into a highlight reel or master class. Now you also have a video product to sell on Amazon Prime Video or Vimeo.

Meditation, Mindfulness, or Technology Detox Retreats and Conferences

A great business idea for a retreat, class or training lies in helping others learn meditation, mindfulness, team building, or offering a technology detox retreat.

People pay big bucks to learn about meditation and mindfulness. If this is something you're an expert in, consider teaching a single day, weekend, or even week-long class or retreat to cover the basics. These retreats work because trying to get started on your own is notoriously difficult. Many people want to become better at mindfulness, as well as taking a digital detox from technology.

Some meditation-style retreats currently have "silent" portions where talking isn't allowed. These retreats are incredibly popular. People pay money to go to a beautiful spot and find peace. You can facilitate that!

_____ *Group Meetups*

Choose a certain group of people and figure out how you can serve them. Let's take a group I'm familiar with: Veterans. There will be over 1,000,000 veterans leaving the military throughout the coming years. There is a massive need for training and retraining for veterans to find great jobs. Whether it's veterans or another group which needs help, consider hosting events for a group or demographic that you know best.

With an example of a veterans' event, I might host an event, conference, or meet-up for veterans. I could charge a small ticket price upfront to ensure people properly value what's being presented and taught. As part of the event, I could offer resume preparation, skill training, and connections to recruiting managers from various employers.

I could call employers who have veteran-hiring initiatives and see if they will sponsor the event. I could initiate a joint venture and create or host events on behalf of a company like HirePurpose. Companies like HirePurpose already have the existing relationships set up with the employers who need talent. Find a company like

HirePurpose in your own niche, and partner with them.

You can act as the intermediary and help them create a great event to bring all parties together. There are many other businesses like this in other industries outside my "veterans" example. What industry do you know best? Create a great event there, and bring together partners who need your help.

Applied Exercises

Before we move on, take a moment to run through these questions. Feel free to jot answers down on a piece of paper. As a quick reminder, the ideal path to absorb and profit from these business ideas is to read along, then write down ideas of your own as you go. As you're reading the ideas in this book, they most likely will spark new ideas. These new ideas are likely based on your past experiences, in which case they might be perfectly suited for you to begin today. Whenever those new ideas are sparked, be sure to write them down immediately!

The questions below aren't listed after every chapter. But as you finish covering the ideas in each chapter, feel free to pause and reflect. The goal of this book is to help you uncover and identify ideas you might be perfectly suited to begin today. By taking the time to reflect on each chapter, you might find you have the resources, connections, or mentors available to start building a business right away. Or, you may find that the questions below (when combined with your experiences) will open up new and better ideas. Whatever the case is, take a moment to consider the questions below:

- Did any of the ideas jump out at you? Why or why not?
- Does any of these ideas fit perfectly with your existing skill?

- If there is an idea you love, but don't have the skills for, how could you go about acquiring the necessary skills? Can you think of the first step?
- Did you find yourself naturally thinking of the next steps you could take to begin some one of these business ideas today?
- Did any of the ideas mentioned jump out, or feel perfectly suited for you? If so, what about them was so appealing?
- Do you have anyone in your network of friends, family, or acquaintances who already runs a business who could help you start one of these ideas? Could you reach out to them, learn from them, help them, or model your business after theirs?
- Did reading these ideas spark any of your own? If they did, be sure to write them down immediately! By the end of the book, be sure to examine any new ideas you've had. These could be the start of business ideas you might be perfectly suited to create and launch.
- Can you envision yourself getting started in one of these areas? Does the thought of getting started pull you forward? Or does it fill you with dread?

- 8 -

Consulting

Incubator or Accelerator

Incubators, co-working spaces, and accelerators are all similar in that they're growing rapidly and need help!

Help out at your local co-working space, incubator or accelerator. If you don't know what they are, do some research and learn about them. The founder of that co-working space, incubator, or accelerator is probably incredibly busy.

Start by reaching out to them and ask how they need help. After you've delivered some value, continue to figure out how you can serve them. Do they need a better way to vet prospective applicants? Do they need help managing everything?

Do they need to find newly established companies to rent space from them? Find out their needs and deliver. Most companies working out of incubators, accelerators, or co-working spaces pay around $300-$400 per person, per month. If they need additional companies to rent space, ask what they are looking for, what they'll pay you for, and what percentage of a contract they'll pay you as a commission for bringing the business to them. This is a great opportunity to be in a place where you can apply to their accelerator, find a great startup to join, or generally just create a great business or job for yourself in a rapidly growing industry.

Help ____ Owned Businesses

Veterans are just one example of a group or demographic of people who are starting businesses in record numbers. There is a big trend towards entrepreneurship in America, and consultants are needed in that space.

Are you part of a demographic or group that you know more about than anyone? You might be in the perfect position to help them start, grow, or expand their businesses. Have you done anything expertly that they need help doing? Can you offer to help them and fix their problems? A great start for a consultant-based business like this is by working for free in exchange for testimonials. Once you've built up enough testimonials and perfected the services you offer, you can charge money for your expertise.

Testimonials

We're living in an era of results. The people who produce, collect, quantify, and display the results and references they achieve will have a very easy time finding work and creating amazing business opportunities for themselves. Not only do people need their results and references collected and displayed, but businesses need this as well. If you can help a business create, quantify and display the results they create as testimonials, you'll help them get more business. By doing this, you'll provide a service that will be in increasing demand.

You can start by creating highly personalized and individualized testimonial videos. You can record videos by just talking and interviewing satisfied customers. On the videos, you can simply introduce yourself and ask the person you're interviewing some questions about their experience at whatever business you're creating the testimonial for. Record their answer and add a branded logo of the company, product, or service at the end. If done right, video testimonials are some of the most underutilized marketing tools available now to businesses. Testimonials help businesses attract more of their ideal customers.

Most businesses unknowingly go out of business because they don't collect enough testimonials, or they don't deliver a good or service that is testimonial-worthy.

Phone and Skype Based Coaching and Consulting

Have you done something that others are paying money to learn right now? Chances are you have. You can use websites like Clarity, which take all the hassle out of consulting for you. Simply set up a profile on a site such as Clarity (https://Clarity.fm) or Live Ninja (https://www.liveninja.com) and you can start getting paid for your expertise.

Fiduciaries

A financial advisor is a thing of the past. Horrible mutual funds that skim off the savings of around 96 million Americans will soon find their client lists dwindling. What will replace them? The answer is simple: index investing and Fiduciaries.

Results-Based Consulting

Take the biggest pain point for everyone in your existing industry and come up with a solution people will pay for. If you correctly learn to identify pain when people or businesses are struggling, you're well on your way to getting paid to remove that pain. If you can remove that bottleneck or hassle through a service you offer, or product you create to solve it, you can become a results-based consultant.

This process starts as simply as interviewing individuals or businesses to find out what they're struggling with. From there, you can find out how you can help them, and you can work with them to figure out what solution they would pay for. Then deliver those solutions, or deliver them for free in exchange for a testimonial to start your own business.

Many people are unnecessarily intimidated by starting a consulting business. To help remove this fear, you can start by helping people for free, in exchange for a testimonial. Simply identify the pain points individuals have for which you can provide a service or counsel to fix. If you remove a true pain point, collecting money for your services becomes a natural by-product. This type of principled pursuit of finding people and helping alleviate their problems by delivering measurable results will never go out of style (or business).

Work With VC Backed Companies

There is a business opportunity waiting for those who can help venture capital backed companies. Many of these companies are so pressed for time that they'll pay money in exchange for completion of immediate odd jobs. Whether this is hunting for office space or acting as a gopher, these businesses are in exciting industries and have a willingness to pay for value.

You can start by finding top-tier VC backed companies. You can study their business models until you discover something they need that you could provide. Or you could call up their founder and ask them what they need help with.

Offer that solution to them and see how they respond. Maybe they need more customers, an event, more hires, etc. Do your homework and research how you can deliver what they need. Deliver first, and then ask to get paid. This is how you can get your foot in the door and land the type of job or consulting gig that never gets advertised. Or you'll build the goodwill necessary to be asked to apply if they do post jobs publicly.

– 9 –

Services, Agencies, and Products

Physical Security

This can start in many different ways, from small jobs to protecting high-net-worth individuals' homes or families. There are also opportunities to teach personalized self-defense or security classes. Work for another company in this pursuit, start your own, or even teach a class about how to be safer on social media (for adolescents, young adults, seniors, etc.). Each age group has its own dangers: sexual predators, bullying, career embarrassment, financial scams. Research what the risks are and what trouble people have gotten into and then figure out how these problems could have been avoided. There are probably thousands of parents who would pay for information on how their kids can be safer and savvier online. Whether it's getting their kids to use CyberDust or another type of app that makes their movements less visible, this is what high-net-worth individuals will pay for. Why has nobody done Uber for security yet?!

Senior and Home Care

Consider that by 2050, it's estimated that Alzheimer's disease will affect over 100 million people.[2] The entire world is aging rapidly, and there is a massive projected shortage in heath care workers and senior care facilities.

You could get started by creating an online site that matches up and offers ratings and reviews on the best nurses and care providers. You could even become one of those providers yourself to learn the industry. Maybe this means you need to get a certification to give you access to this field. After you get certified, you can build a business that helps this massive and growing need all across the world.

The global population is aging quickly, and the number of diseases and ailments of an aging population means high demand for compassionate businesses and caretakers.

Hiring and Staffing

Start your own service hiring or staffing business. You can begin by finding businesses that need specific jobs filled.

Then go on LinkedIn and introduce them to qualified candidates. Hiring and turnover are two huge expenses for businesses. By improving and reducing those two, respectively, you can create an amazing business for yourself.

Staffing, headhunting and employment services are a multi-billion dollar industry, and can be extremely lucrative in fields like technology. In addition to staffing, you could help bring in customer, partner, or joint venture opportunities for the businesses you work with.

Apprentice to a Serial Entrepreneur

Become an apprentice to a serial entrepreneur. The quickest way to start your own business is to be around other people who have. This might not seem like a business at first, but the knowledge or accelerated learning you might be privy to will quickly set you on a path of mastery. Not many people are willing to go find the best in the world in a particular field and learn directly from them. Conversely, this is probably the best place to look to learn how to build a business of your own. Go work for a serial entrepreneur; listen, endure, stay humble, and you'll inevitably build the skill sets and knowledge of marketplaces to leave and start a business.

Apprentice to a Pro

Reach out to someone online whose work you enjoy, whose ideas resonate with you, and work for him or her. The best teachers in the world aren't in the classroom. They're busy doing, and relaying when they can. This doesn't mean you'll necessarily be a VA or intern, but rather a happy medium of just being ridiculously helpful while learning under someone whose ideas impress you, or is dominating the industry they're in.

Holiday Helping Service

A holiday helper on hand helps create and facilitate great holiday experiences. Whether it's a birthday, Christmas, Halloween, Thanksgiving, Easter, or an anniversary, create a great service-based business around helping others get ready for the holidays.

Life Skills

Life Skills Class: teaching English, reading, and writing to immigrants. Between now and 2050, 68 million immigrants will be coming to the United States. The rest of the world is learning English. Help teach them. They'll happily pay money to learn more effectively. You can sell the byproducts of your work online, host events, etc. There are many opportunities for this.

High-End Electronic Repair

High-end electronics will need repairs. Plenty of people just got iPhone 6's and didn't buy insurance. They'll need somebody who can repair them after the fourth time they drop them. Whether you start with the iPhone 6 or top of the line drones, robotic toys, or Nest censors (the Internet of things), high-end electronics will need skilled technicians on hand.

Many people will buy expensive drones, and few will understand how to fix them or be able to resell them. Create a service around fixing high-end electronics, or create a marketplace where hobbyists can sell them. Big firms might sell well online, but few will be able to offer local technical repair services. That's where you come in.

Cooking Class

Let's be honest. Most people don't cook that often. Cooking classes are exploding in popularity at places like Whole Foods, but this doesn't mean you can't host a cooking class or even full meal as an event. Many people are starting to host their own unique cooking dinners. They'll sell tickets to 20 friends at $30-$40 apiece, and create a dining experience. That type of dinner with a big group of friends is hard to buy at any restaurant, and many people who love to cook are finding they can deliver a meal for others in an enjoyable, and intimate fashion. Plus, they often find they can do it for cheaper than a restaurant!

Skills and Trades

Skills and trades like plumbing, welding, and technical manufacturing are soaring in demand. For those interested in starting a business crucial to everyone, and pays well, look no further than skills and trades. Celebrities like Mike Rowe have become well known for tirelessly promoting all the jobs and careers that few people want to do. Because these jobs are not glamorous, they are undervalued in the marketplace. This means there is an increasing premium being offered for those who can do them well. With minimal experience, many plumbers who start their own businesses make just as much money as doctors! Unknown to many people, medical personal and doctors have their careers at risk from technologies on the horizon like consumer medical diagnostic devices. While these white-collar professionals have their careers threatened, many blue collar professions will enjoy high wages far out in the future. To examine the best routes to start a business in a vocational skill or trade, you can check out places like MikeRowe.com or the BLS Occupational Outlook Handbook.

– 10 –

Location Independent Opportunities

Adobe Creative Suite Master

For those who are artistically or design inclined, consider mastering the Adobe Creative Suite. Whether it's Photoshop, Illustrator, or audio and video production, masters of the Adobe Creative Suite can always find work. You can advertise your work or services everywhere from Craigslist to Fiverr, oDesk, Elance, Dribble, Bechance, or Envato Studio. There is an endless stream of businesses which need skilled designers who can leverage technology to create multimedia masterpieces.

High-End Designer

Once you perfect your design skills, you can consider offering your services as a high-end designer. Instead of offering your services everywhere, you can consider only searching for leads in specific locations or areas.

Or you could focus your expertise on doing work in a specific area, with a big ability to pay. Maybe you become the world's best designer in the medical device field. This is a niche where the competition is low and the willingness to pay is high.

If you're an amazing designer and you know it, the best strategy is to start with high-end clients and deliver amazing work.

Front End Web and App Developer

There is location independent work for any design professional who masters user interface and user experience design, and development. When you layer the ability to develop web apps with decent design skills, you'll have a stream of clients lining up for your services.

There are many training programs to get started as a developer, including one-month to four-month-long classes where you can learn these skills.

Full Stack Marketer

"Full Stack Marketer" is a term for the technically skilled marketer of the 21st century. Maybe you've heard this person or skill set referred to as a "growth hacker." The terms growth hacker and full stack marketer are simply terms for marketers who know how to use technology, data and analytics to do great work and produce results for clients.

Marketing and business masters like Jay Abraham have been doing full stack or growth hacker marketing for years. This simply means they make decisions based on quantitative metrics instead of emotions. Jay is the "original gangster" of growth hacking. For anyone interested in becoming a growth hacker, you can learn the technical skills, and then blend them with the classic tried and true approaches of folks like Jay Abraham. After which, you'll be well on your way to becoming a full stack marketer whose services will always be in demand.

Tyler Cowen, in his excellent book <u>Average is Over</u>, confirms that competent technical marketing/sales/business development will continue to be fiercely in demand now and in the future. I couldn't agree more; those who can help existing businesses make more money will always have jobs, opportunity, and the ability to work remotely.

Learn everything about growth hacking. Find some online marketers and get started buying media and advertisements for their products. From there you can begin acquiring other skills such as creating advertisements, writing sales copy, purchasing traffic/app installs/ downloads, and generally acquiring customers through careful number crunching. Learning metric-based marketing, creating viral loops, and presenting quantitative results in an easy to understand visual story is the perfect route for anyone interested in starting a 21st century marketing businesses.

Mobile / Swift Developer

The number one remote skill set in demand right now is for Mobile iOS developers. The new Apple programming language Swift has made it easier than ever to begin learning. You can get started by learning Swift and Xcode for iOS, and from there you can learn Appfolio in order to port Swift apps to Android.

Full Stack Developer

Another remote business opportunity is to become a full stack developer. This is a developer who has knowledge of the front end, model layer, and back end of software applications. You can get started by going to a boot camp to learn these skills, or start learning online right now. You can expand this skill set into an agency with services for clients or build your own products.

Data Scientists

It's estimated that by 2018, the data generated from the "Internet of things" will be over 400 zettabytes PER YEAR of data (1 zettabyte = a trillion gigabytes).

Wow. It sounds like data scientists will be in big demand!

For those consultants who start in the data arena, their future prospects are incredibly bright. These aspiring data scientists can get started by mastering Excel, HTML, R-Studio, writing scripts, learning Hadoop and Javascript, and generally just becoming a master at understanding and sifting through data. They can combine this knowledge with a tool like Wolfram Alpha to start a lucrative consulting business where they can work remotely, or build an agency which does larger scale work for bigger clients.

Quality Control

Performing quality control work, or becoming a technical proofreader, is a freelancing or consulting based business opportunity that will boom in our digital age.

If you have a fastidious attention to detail or are a great editor, there is a huge demand for your consulting services on oDesk and Elance.

This type of editing and quality control work can quickly expand into an agency, or you can get a few clients and make a very comfortable income.

You can use oDesk, Elance or Envato Studio to get started, or any other service oriented marketplace platform. You could set up a personal website to portray your past work and a professional appearance, and then put ads on Craigslist or local bulletin boards for your services.

Quick Technical Gigs

Fiverr is a freelancing site where workers perform a variety of tasks for $5. By studying this site and determining what you can offer quickly and competently, you can make a great living. How you ask?

The genius in Fiverr is not in the $5 services, but in the multiple up-sells that you're encouraged to offer clients. Many up-sells include services which are expansions on the first $5 gig. For example, you might edit the first 300 words for someone for $5, and for $20 more you'll do 1,500 words, and for $40 more you'll edit 5,000 words.

A few of those up-sells add up! If you perform just ten $5 gigs a day, it's only $50. But if you can do ten $5 gigs and land just three $40 up-sells, now you're talking about $180 a day, plus the ability to work from anywhere.

Researcher for a Prolific Author

Do you know an author who is prolific? Chances are they need a skilled researcher. If you're very technically savvy and can use the Internet well, being a researcher for a prolific author is a great potential freelancing gig.

You can begin by demonstrating the level at which you can work and deliver. You can work a bit for free, and then charge soon after. You can build up a portfolio of work or do work for several authors at once. You can even leverage your work up the chain and work for authors who are progressively more famous or widely known. Along the way, you can sell other services or handle virtual assistant duties as the need arises, or as you identify a pain point in your client's business.

Celebrity Apprentice

There are thousands of micro-celebrities online now who need talented virtual assistants to handle daily tasks such as email, comments, editing, appointments, and scheduling. Reach out to them and work with them.

Quarterly Aggregator

Quarterly.co is a company that sends out boxes packed with interesting stuff from celebrities once a quarter or monthly. There are now several big names on Quarterly who you could reach out to, offering to help sort and create their boxes. Or you could reach out to several smaller, lesser-known celebrities in the same niche or market, and offer to put a box together for them.

– 11 –

Teaching, Curation, and Media

Teach a Hobby

What's your hobby? How do you stay fit and healthy? Consider teaching your hobby to others who want to learn. Whether it's paddle boarding, snowboarding, or whatever you're so good at that others have complimented you on, teach that to others! You can create and sell tickets through platforms like Eventbrite or PayPal. You can ask your friends, co-workers, or those who have complimented your abilities or skill to buy tickets to your first teaching event!

Coaching Local Sports

Many local sports teams in middle and high school pay for great coaches. Why not take a sport you are passionate about and teach it to others? This is a great opportunity to be a mentor to young people and help them develop a passion for health and fitness.

Media Show, Radio, or Podcast

If there is a subject you love talking about, consider hosting a new media, radio, or podcast show.

You can simply chat about whatever industry you're interested in. You can create content by interviewing every major player in the space. This could start as a podcast with audio only, and then slowly transition to video.

Ninety million Americans commute to work every morning and are looking for great entertaining, educational, or inspiring content to lift them up. There are many distribution channels available through which you can reach them. These include iTunes, Stitcher, Sirus XM, YouTube, Vimeo, Soundcloud, Google Play, Roku, and the Amazon Store. If you can create a great show with information that people need and want, you'll be able to get advertisers or figure out a way to turn it into a powerful business.

Sell the By-Products

Sell the by-products of being entrepreneurial. If you set up or design your own website, or have a great LinkedIn or AngelList profile, consider offering that to others who want it. Maybe you've learned how to set up a Shopify store. You can help others do that and get paid for doing it.

What might be easy for you to do may feel impossible to others. There will always be a market of busy people who will pay for others to do tasks for them.

News and Media Publication

You can start a news or media publication using a Wordpress news magazine template or using Squarespace. Don't start a personal blog unless you're a creator, public speaker or CEO who will use that site to get clients. Starting a news site in an industry you want to learn more about is a turnkey way to open up the opportunities you want. An example might be in a growing industry like big data.

You could start a news site on big data jobs, or big data news where you profile how to break into big data, follow and comment on industry trends, or link interested people with the training necessary to begin working with big data.

You can find existing bloggers and experts on the topic on which you're building your news site. Many of them already have content they need to reprise. Just ask them if they want to repurpose it, and publish it on your site.

Once your website starts getting traffic, you can create a job listing page and charge employers to place their job listings on your site. You can even further serve them by trying to find employees for them.

There are still many websites and news sites ready to be created in relatively new and booming industries such as RPAS, Bitcoin, Energy, Fracking, IT Security, Programming/Coding, Consulting, Freelancing, Elder Care, and Franchises.

Find service companies which are leading the way in these industries and figure out the type of customers they need. Determine what types of questions customers who might use these businesses are asking. Start answering the questions customers have about the niche (or vertical) you're in, and point them in the direction of the service provider you partner with. This is a content site that can make money very quickly. You can monetize through affiliates, hiring, or even selling digital training courses.

Niche News Site

We covered some larger examples of a business idea for a media news site. Let's niche that idea down even further. An extreme niche site where there is little to no competition might be the best place to start. A great example of this might be a hyper specific subset of an existing vertical. So maybe you're a teacher who teaches English as a second language. Instead of a teaching news site, start an EASL website devoted to teachers just like you.

You can aggregate and cover news and the latest details in your specific niche. You can insert a pop-up to help you collect email addresses. You can create a great course for that space and sell it through a series of email auto-responders.

Teaching an Online Class

What do you know that you could package and teach as a single class? If there is a skill you have that you're enthusiastic about, consider teaching it online. There are many platforms ready for you to offer your class right now. Whether it's on a platform like Udemy, Skillshare, GumRoad, or Fedora, teach what you know and love to others.

Public Speaking

Did you know that some public speakers make thousands to hundreds of thousands of dollars for a single speech? There are skilled public speakers that make full time incomes from speaking alone. There are topics people will always pay to hear. Some of these include topics such as tips and advice on relationships, how to make money, getting in better shape, or finding work they're passionate about.

All you have to do is find out what other people want that you love speaking about. Then speak about that. You can use a platform like Orate.me to get started charging for your speeches.

There is a huge demand from conference and event groups for public speakers who can actively engage with audiences. If you can think on your feet, make jokes, and teach while being semi-entertaining, there is a great service to provide through public speaking.

Personal Standardized Test and Credentials Tutor

The test preparation market for standardized tests and certifications is over $1 billion in size.

There is always a business opportunity in helping tutor and train people to excel at these tests and certifications. If you can achieve a great score on a standardized test like the SAT, ACT, GRE, ASVAB, LSAT or MCAT, you can likely start a business teaching others how to do the same.

After you get a great score on one of these tests, simply break that down into a teachable format, create a class around it, and offer that class. You can get started by offering it for free, recording the event, and playing the video to sell tickets for the next one.

There are thousands, if not tens of thousands, of people who would pay to ensure they do well at whatever test they're taking. Whether you limit your teaching to an in-person class, a book, a digital course, or an event, there is always a test preparation market waiting for better results.

Online Tutor

In addition to offering your services as a standardized test preparation and results master, you can become an online tutor. Instead of teaching those methods in person, teach them online in a way which allows you to teach many people at once, or teach groups of people at their own pace.

If you think there isn't a market for online tutors and teaching for your specific interest, you might be wrong. A great example of this is Sean Wes. He teaches and tutors people in how to draw lettering by hand. If you're a creative type, this is a fantastic way to share and sell the by-products of your work in a way that gets your name out there.

Social Media

There will always be a new social media platform which businesses need to utilize more efficiently. Learn new platforms and then help businesses train their employees on how to use them.

Ideally, start by helping a business which is willing to pay or is willing to refer you to other businesses which will. Start an agency that helps a specific type of business or professional on social media.

High End Newsletter or Subscription

There are several premium news sites and newsletters which cost big bucks to subscribe to. The publishers of those newsletters are working in hyper-specific market niches and are able to charge premium prices because of their expertise.

If you think there aren't many sites that do this, guess again. Many expensive subscriptions such as the Financial Times, Wall Street Journal, or specific legal journals, cost several hundred or thousands of dollars a year. Find the premium journal that isn't being created, but that firms will pay for. A Bitcoin trading newsletter, cyber security, or deep learning newsletter come to mind as great ideas.

Preventive Care

With health insurance costs skyrocketing, there is a huge need for those who can train others in proper preventive care. This industry will continue to explode. Many big employers are working hard to measure how well their employees do or do not take care of themselves. This brings up a big need and willingness to pay to create a business that teaches people how to monitor their sleep, eat healthy (no sugar, no gluten), measure the air quality of their home, track their vital signs through their FitBit or Jawbone device, and offer them meaningful solutions.

Then, your health and preventive care business can even be expanded to offer healthy shopping as a service, prepared meals as a service, or monthly checkups to keep your clients on track.

Not only is this an opportunity that you can work with individuals on, but partnering with corporations is another angle one can take with this business. Healthy employees mean lower health care costs, and happier corporations.

- 12 -

Go Forth and Conquer!

Conclusion

If you've made it this far, congratulations! I hope these 100 business ideas were an enjoyable read. The most exciting part of these ideas is you can begin many of them today. But the most difficult part of getting started happens when you're in the idea phase. The path that any new idea has to travel, from inception to realization, can be treacherous. The second we think of a new idea, we have a tendency to criticize them. Our survival instincts are still strong, and sadly they tend to strangle new ideas and ventures before they can begin. The same risk exists anytime we run our new ideas by anyone around us; those ideas are likely to be critiqued and criticized before they can begin. The only, "safe" person to run new ideas by or collaborate with are others who are entrepreneurial, or full-time entrepreneurs.

I wish I could say that starting a business or building a side stream of income was easy. But of course it's not. If anyone tells you it's easy, you might want to run! The magic of this pursuit lies in the fact that it's not easy. It's in the pursuit, and the journey of creating a business that we tend to find ourselves. Because the pursuit is so difficult, it tends to help mold those who stay the course. The hard truth is that as long as you never stop trying and learning, there is no failure. The truth is hard because success is available to only those who will not quit. By accepting that truth, we cut off retreat. Yes, we occasionally may have to regroup, but deep down, we'll know that giving up is foolish. Winston Churchill said it best, "never, never, never, give up." If you don't give up, and keep learning as you go, you will eventually build a side stream of income, or maybe even a full-fledged business. The magic of the pursuit is, you'll never know until you get started!

Maybe you've heard the saying that ideas are worthless. That's an over-simplified and cliche saying. It's not specific enough to mean anything.

The truth about ideas is, they are both worthless and priceless at the same time. Ideas can be incredibly valuable (if you execute on them) or they can be completely worthless (and even maddening) if you do nothing but sit on them. If you've read this far, I'm betting that you're the type who executes on them.

I hope that as you've been reading, one or more of these many ideas has jumped out at you. Maybe you have a background perfectly suited to get started working to turn that idea into a business? Or better yet, maybe after reading all of these ideas, your mind has begun generating better ideas! In either case, don't hesitate to get started! When you do, remember that 99% of people will never even begin. If you have the courage to begin, you've already set yourself apart from the pack.

Most people who seek to start businesses or side streams of income fail because they don't continually generate new ideas. The professional or the entrepreneur who succeeds is always developing new ideas. They are always building up their imagination by writing down new ideas, filtering old ones, delegating next steps, or executing on new ideas. They are always working to turn what is in their imagination into objective fact.

Don't be afraid to start very small. Remember that it's a marathon, and not a sprint. Small steps, taken every day, are better than taking none at all. So, no matter where you're at, write down some ideas for the first steps you could take today. There is power in baby steps. Don't ever be ashamed of getting started in a ridiculously small way. In fact, it requires serious courage and belief in yourself to trust in humble steps.

Maybe you send out a single email. Maybe you post an add on craigslist for one of the services mentioned here. Whatever you do, just please don't be afraid to start. Whether you use one of the ideas included in this book or you decide to start developing and executing on your own, remember that ideas only "work" to the extent that you do!

As you go forth, remember that we don't learn until we

take action. We might remember these ideas, or even generate new ones, but our learning can't accelerate until we blend ideas, action, and time for reflection. Once we cycle through this type of action, we become good at learning how to learn. And that is the ultimate skill of the 21st century.

Whenever I'm getting ready to take the next step and begin a new idea, I'll usually feel lazy. Or, I'll criticize the idea in my head and wonder, "who am I to begin such a project?" When this happens, I calmly ask myself a few simple questions – "At the end my life, will I regret not taking the first step? Do I even know where this idea could lead? What if it leads to something more amazing than I can even imagine right now? Will I regret not exploring this idea today?" These are a few of the questions that fire me up to take action and get started. Maybe they'll be useful for you too.

No matter where you're at, I thank you for taking the time to read this book. When you turn this page, Amazon will ask you if you'd like to leave a review for this book. If you've found any value here and could leave a review, I would greatly appreciate it!

At the beginning of this book, we talked about many business icons, and how they each got started. Remember that they all got started just like you, taking small steps that from the outside looked trivial. They didn't get to where they are by thinking about how small the steps were they were taking. They got to where they are by never being afraid to get started, by constantly generating new ideas, and with the help of luck and positivity along the way. If you can respect whatever small start you take today, I have no doubt that you'll be well on your way to building a business or side stream of income. Thank you for reading, and best of luck as you go forth and conquer! Enjoy the journey.

Endnotes

1. https://usefedora.com
2. Perlmutter, David (2013-09-17). Grain Brain: The Surprising Truth about Wheat, Carbs, and Sugar--Your Brain's Silent Killers (p. 31). Little, Brown and Company. Kindle Edition.

www.ingramcontent.com/pod-product-compliance
Lightning Source LLC
Chambersburg PA
CBHW051916170526
45168CB00001B/419